ALL OF THE ABOVE

ESSAYS ON TEACHING ENGLISH AS A FOREIGN LANGUAGE

DOROTHY ZEMACH

WAYZGOOSE PRESS

Copyright © 2022 by Dorothy Zemach

All rights reserved.

No part of this book may be reproduced in any form or by any electronic or mechanical means, including information storage and retrieval systems, without written permission from the author, except for the use of brief quotations in a book review.

Note: Several of these essays were originally published on AzarGrammar.com.

CONTENTS

1. Drilling for Language — 1
2. Why I Teach the Parts of Speech — 6
3. Yo, yo, sup dude — 12
4. In Praise of Praise — 17
5. Can a Teacher Motivate Every Student? — 22
6. Should Learning English Be Fun? — 27
7. Modeling Student Talk — 32
8. Teaching Pre-Reading Skills — 38
9. Advice to a Young Iranian English Teacher — 43
10. Elevator Pitch — 48
11. May I Have a Copy of Your Presentation? — 52
12. A Sick Policy? — 57
13. Should Students Use a Grammar Checker? — 62
14. My Dear — 74
15. She Was in a Lift with a Priest Who Sneezed — 85

16. THE PLACE OF GAMES IN THE LANGUAGE CLASSROOM
   Board Games — 95
   Flyswatters — 103
   Concentration — 110

1

DRILLING FOR LANGUAGE

The first time I studied a foreign language was in 5th grade, when my family lived in Geneva, Switzerland. My brother and I attended a private school where we essentially learned French all day, except when we were pulled out for sewing and needlework (girls) or shop (boys) or sports (everyone).

Fresh off the plane, my brother and I began at the beginning: the alphabet, simple greetings, numbers, colors, then verb conjugations.

We completed one lesson in the textbook each day, and the next day were called individually to the blackboard to take a quiz, either oral or written on the board. We were graded instantly, in front of the class.

Classwork consisted mainly of copying out verb conjugations a number of times, completing written exercises, memorizing vocabulary lists, and answering surprise drill questions fired out by the teacher when we least expected it.

Life in the 'Language Lab'

Every now and then we went off to a dark little room—I guess some precursor to the "language lab"—where we'd watch filmstrips that advanced one frame at a time. A slide would come up, we'd listen to the French, repeat it in chorus, and *beep*! The next slide would come.

Years later, when I was in graduate school, it seemed fashionable to mock the audio-lingual method, rote memorization, drills, choral repetitions, and the teacher-centered classroom. Certainly a lot of what people were saying about a student-centered, communicative classroom did sound more appealing. A gentler, more human approach. Empowering. And yet... and yet... I *did* learn French, fluently. You could argue that some of that could have been due to my being 11 and living in a French-speaking environment for five months. But to this day I remember those filmstrips down to the word—and that was 34 years ago (oh, go ahead, do the math, I don't mind).

Où est-ce que vous habitez, Jacques? (*beep*!)
J'habite rue de la Poste (*beep*!)
En face du cinéma. (*beep*!)

And yes, I have the accent and intonation down too. A frequent criticism of the audio-lingual method is that students can't substitute freely and correctly with the patterns to make original sentences; yet that certainly wasn't true for me or my brother.

More Fun, Less Learning

Japanese was my second foreign language. I studied for one semester at a college in Oregon. Our teacher had us memorize a dialogue every day, practice repeatedly with a partner, and recite it in class the next day for a grade. Later, in Japan, I took classes that were much more communicative. And while they were more fun, I never seemed to make any actual progress with learning the language. Even after living there for five years, the vocabulary and patterns I know best are those I learned in the US from constant drilling and memorization.

I later watched my husband struggle with his Japanese class. "What do you want to learn?" asked the teacher. My husband asked for a lesson on food because he was in charge of the grocery shopping. The teacher obligingly handed out a list of what must have been every vegetable ever eaten in Japan, as well as many that have never crossed its shores, and then asked the class (in Japanese), "What are your favorite dishes?" Of course no one could answer, since no one knew the words "favorite" or "dishes," let alone how to describe them using only a list of ingredients. The class continued with more "discussion questions" about food, and my husband came home very frustrated.

The Payoff Is Worth the Price

I asked him what he would have preferred. He said (yes, my husband Mr. Visual Learner and General Touchy-Feely Guy) that he would have liked a few short dialogues to memorize and then to have recited them for the entire lesson, doing just simple substitutions, until he had the material memorized cold. He conceded that it would have been dull—but said the payoff of learning the material would have been more than worth it.

Now, I'm not advocating a boring classroom, or saying there's no place for open-ended discussion or even "free conversation." But I do think that when communicative language teaching came into fashion, the baby might have been thrown out with the bathwater. If our students want to learn English, then really, what is going to please them most is actually learning English—even if that means some drills, repetitions, and memorization, or even the teacher leading the class sometimes (imagine!). I don't underestimate the part a relaxed and enjoyable classroom atmosphere can play in a student's mood and motivation. However, it's OK to trade some momentary fun in class today for students really knowing some language at the end of the course.

Food for thought: Think of your first experience learning a foreign language. What method was used? Did it work for you? Why or why not? How you can you use what was done to you to inform your own teaching?

2

WHY I TEACH THE PARTS OF SPEECH

Actually, I wanted to write about phrases and clauses and about teaching them as adjectives and adverbs. However, that reminded me how many teachers I've run into over the years who disagree that the names of parts of speech should be taught to students. I argued with a publisher over this for at least three years, actually, before being "allowed" to teach the parts of speech in a textbook for lower-level students. So let me take a brief diversion to defend this position.

The arguments against teaching the names of the parts of speech are mainly that the terms are too difficult for students to learn, and further, that they aren't helpful. I disagree with both of these arguments.

Minimally, I think students should know *noun, pronoun, verb, adjective, adverb, preposition,* and *article*. With advanced students I might add in *determiner*. OK, that's seven words. Is that too high a vocabulary load, especially when most of those concepts exist in the learner's native language? I think if they can learn seven objects in the classroom, or seven modes of transportation, or seven irregular verbs, then seven parts of speech isn't going to short out the brain.

A larger issue is whether they're helpful. This depends, of course, on whether the teacher uses the labels. I use them all the time. I use them to talk about

- different word forms (*accept* is a verb; *acceptance* is the noun form of that verb);
- the placement of different parts of speech (*Your sentence "Is late again" is missing a noun or a pronoun as the subject*); and
- the functions of subordinate clauses and prepositional phrases and so on.

It seems to me that one of the challenges of forming correct and elegant sentences in English is in knowing where to put the different elements. Where does the subject go? Where does the verb go? How about the direct object? And those are the easier things to teach.

Where my more advanced students trip up is in knowing where to put longer elements, such as

- *in the morning*
- *running for the bus*
- *while on his way to the bakery*
- *on the corner*

The problem is that students don't know what these elements are—that is, how they function. Therefore, they can't place them correctly in a sentence.

Pretty much, they're adjectives and adverbs—more correctly called adjectivals and adverbials, but I use *adjective phrase* and *adverb phrase* with my students at first, and then just *adjective* and *adverb*, once we're all on the same page.

Suppose we have a simple sentence:

He fell.

Even lower-level students have probably seen the structure subject + verb + adverb, and might be able to write a sentence such as

*He fell **slowly**.*

However, the most common adverbs are actually NOT the one-word ones that end with ~ly, even though those are the easiest ones to identify. An adverb tells us where, when, why, or how. If students know that phrases can be used to talk about when, where, why, or how, then they can write

*He fell **to the ground**.*
*He fell **when he tripped**.*
*He fell **as soon as he tried to stand up**.*
*He fell **with a strange choking sound**.*

The trick is in knowing that *to the ground* (where?) functions as an adverb, as do *when he tripped* (when?) and *as soon as he tried to* stand up (both when? and why?) and *with a strange choking sound* (how?). English allows (and even encourages!) one to combine adverb phrases and clauses, as in

*He fell **to the ground with a strange choking sound as soon as he tried to stand up**.*

Getting this concept down is huge. It doesn't bother me terribly much if a student writes

*He fell at the ground.

or

*He fell as soon as tried to stand up.

Those sentences contain errors, of course, but the basic pattern of subject + verb + adverb is still there.

Adverbs are movable elements, more so than most others. But students need to know that adverb clauses and phrases move as units, and where they move to—for instance, to the beginning of a sentence:

As soon as he tried to stand up, *he fell.*

To take another example: A student who is writing short, careful, simple sentences and wishes to expand them might wish to add some adjectives. Students are usually taught simple one-word adjectives (that answer the question What kind of? or Which?) that come before a noun.

She went to the bakery.
*She went to the **new** bakery.*

But how much more interesting if we can describe the bakery with some prepositional phrases; note that these come after the noun:

*She went to the bakery **on the corner**.*
*She went to the bakery **with the jumbo strawberry creampuffs**.*

Again, an error in choosing the correct preposition doesn't bother me if the student is able to modify the noun with a phrase.

This is the way I like to address syntax, especially in reading and writing, with at least intermediate and advanced students—and some beginners as well. And that is why my very lowest level students learn the names of the parts of speech—so that we can talk about what the parts of speech are and how they function.

Food for thought: Think of textbooks you use now or have used recently. Do they name any parts of speech? If not, where could you insert this sort of instruction? Can you think of any fun activities (i.e., Mad Libs) that would help teach the parts of speech?

3

YO, YO, SUP DUDE

Writing used to be one of the hardest skills for learners to practice on their own outside of class, back in the Dark Days before email and the Internet. Options were basically limited to keeping a written journal or exchanging letters and postcards with a pen pal and the occasional "letter to the newspaper" classroom assignment.

Now, however, opportunities to freely practice writing abound: keypals, social networking sites, bulletin boards, chat rooms, websites where customers leave reviews and comments, blogs, and so on.

So… writing skills must have vastly improved, right? Well, perhaps a certain degree of fluency has. However, what we also have is a host of new problems. You're teaching a class the difference between *two*, *too*, and *to*, and then they come in wanting to spell all of them 2.

I think there are two basic problems: the models students see and the attitudes they can pick up towards writing.

Poor Writing Models Abound Online

Certainly the level of writing they could encounter from native speakers out there in Internetland is something of a concern. Masses of writers seem unaware of (or unconcerned about) differences between your and you're, or loose and lose, or (a pet peeve of mine) our and are. Misspellings are rampant, even in these days when most Internet browsers have a built-in spellcheck feature. Posters, even of longer blogs, may eschew punctuation and even capitalization. If students then are answering with the same language they see, we can expect similar mistakes, or at least a lot of confusion.

Texting Shorthand: Easier for Whom?

A bigger problem though is writers (native English speaker or otherwise) who simply don't care. *It's only an Internet message board,* a perpetrator might say, *not an English class.* Writers who use texting shorthand point out that it's faster. Faster to write, yes, if one is used to that. But faster to read? I don't think so, especially not when sloppy writing and no punctuation between sentences obscures meaning. If you didn't communicate what you intended, then your message failed, even if you got it out there in cyberspace extra fast.

The choice then that writers make is whether to make things easier on themselves or easier on their reader. Unless the message being written is truly a personal journal (in which case, why is it online?), there's usually some reason to communicate to readers—to express an opinion, ask a question, give information, ask for help. It's even likely that there will be multiple readers of messages, in which case I tell students that, as Mr. Spock would put it, "The needs of the many outweigh the needs of the one." At first, students are surprised to hear that writing sloppily is selfish; but give them some time to consider the idea, and you'd be surprised how many would agree.

It may not be an English class, but aren't online writers in some sense being graded? They're certainly being judged. I can take a certain amount of informality online, but when spelling and typing errors get to a certain level, I just skip over the messages without even trying to read them.

It's even more important to me that emails sent directly

to me be clear and careful. A student who's getting a grade from me in an English class isn't going to look good by sending *yo yo sup dude did u get my homwork im pretty sur i sent it b4*. If you think teachers don't get emails like this, check in with a high school teacher (of any subject) sometime. However, students can't know what level of formality you expect if you don't tell them directly. Merely copying what native speaker classmates are doing isn't necessarily going to steer them in the right direction.

Writers are also challenged by autocorrect and autocomplete errors, as well as simply typing mistakes. It's faster to leave these uncorrected—faster for the writer. But, as with abbreviations and lack of punctuation, slower for the reader. I'm *not* advocating that everybody texting fix every autocorrect error and put in every apostrophe. But I am advocating that writers (whether students or not) consider their audience and their purpose every time they write—even if it's a short, simple message. How "correct" you are when you write is a choice; so make sure you know what choice you are making and why!

Appropriate Use of Informal Writing Needs to be Taught

I don't see many teaching materials that address informal writing except to say not to use it. That's also a mistake, though. Any community has its own discourse, of course, and being overly formal in a chat room isn't going to be successful either. There's a world of difference between *kthnxbai* and *Please accept my sincere thanks for all of your assistance*.

Students need explicit instruction to know what levels of language exist and when to use them. If you don't have examples and materials, don't worry—ask your students to bring you examples of written English from different Internet sites that they visit. Ask them to find English that they believe is the most correct and appropriate, as well as the least correct and appropriate, and then share and discuss the examples in class. Collect similar examples when you're online and keep them in a file. Ask students what impressions they have of the writers and to what extent those impressions are formed by the language and the place in which it appears. Compile a class glossary of the common abbreviations and expressions they encounter online and code each one as appropriate for class or not.

And don't forget to point out that they will never be disadvantaged by being better able to switch between informal and formal English than their native speaker friends.

Food for thought: Think about different people you email and message. With whom are you the most informal? the most formal? Do you ever proofread messages before you send them? If so, what would you say to a learner who asked you why you do that?

4

IN PRAISE OF PRAISE

My son is a good writer. I remember when he became one, back in 6th grade—when his teacher told him he was one. He hadn't really written much at that point, so she was just going on her instincts—she could see he loved to read, and his spelling and grammar were decent, and he did have a tendency to ramble on, when writing as well as when speaking.

He'd never minded writing before, but equally didn't find it especially appealing; it was just something one did in school. However, once his teacher told him he was a good writer, he took that on. He spent more time on his assignments and he tried harder. He even said he felt he had to do better than the other kids in his class "because she expects it of me. I'm a good writer." Not surprisingly, through increased effort, he really did become a good writer, a skill that stayed with him throughout high school.

Such a simple thing to say to a child: "You're a good writer." And yet what an impact it had. A well-placed comment like that can change the shape of someone's education, and, by extension, their career and their future.

Of course, we can't just tell all of the learners in our classroom that they are good writers and then stand back and watch it come true. For praise to be meaningful, it has to be said 1) with sincerity and 2) at the right time.

Praise that rings false is worse than no praise at all, and students are adept at knowing when you're saying something you don't really believe. Even if false praise is believed, it isn't helpful because it gives students inaccurate information. Telling a student her pronunciation is excellent when actually she is practically unintelligible will (if she doesn't believe you) lead her to think you're making fun of her or don't believe she can ever get any better, or (if she believes you) keep her from working towards necessary improvements.

Praise at the right time means praise when a student is

open to hearing it and could use an affirmation or an encouragement. I think there's something special about anticipatory praise, too, like my son got—he hadn't won a Pulitzer prize for writing at that time, and in fact, being 11, hadn't done much writing at all. But his teacher sensed his potential, and, in effect, praised that—creating a self-fulfilling prophecy. I think a lot of us can remember a time in our academic lives when, feeling just a bit uncertain about our talents or unsure of ourselves, and some authority figure or someone we looked up to gave us the right words of encouragement.

It's not always easy to praise students. Sometimes we don't know them very well. Sometimes they're actually not doing very well. Sometimes other students demand more of our time.

I've found that many teachers, being compassionate and nurturing, actually pay more attention to those students who are struggling. Of course, this is a wonderful thing to do. And yet—I think it's important not to overlook the students who are doing well. It's shortchanging them to think that good test scores and grades are reward enough. Remember that "good" students can have as many insecurities and moments of self-doubt as the outwardly less successful.

I'll close by describing an activity I've often done with classes at the end of a semester or term—although there's no reason you couldn't do it in the middle of a course either.

1. Have students sit in a circle, if your numbers and room space allow; otherwise, they can keep their

regular seats, but a circle where they can all make eye contact is nice.
2. Choose one student to start, and have her (or him) thank the person on her left for something concrete. Give a few examples at the start so students get the idea—"Thank you for giving me the homework assignments when I forgot to copy them down" or "Thank you for making me laugh in class" or "Thank you for letting me use your dictionary."
3. The person receiving the compliment says "You're welcome," and turns to the person on his left and gives a compliment, and so on around the circle.

Note that everyone gives and receives a compliment, and that students don't choose whom they speak to (it's just determined by seating order). I promise that you will be amazed, as well as touched, by the things students mention! I've done this with high school students, university students, businessmen, mixed groups of adults and teens... and there are always a few people moved to tears. If you can't always praise your students, then, let them praise each other.

Food for thought: How often do you praise your students? Do you have a system for making sure that praise is distributed more or less evenly? What was the most impactful praise you ever received from a teacher?

5

CAN A TEACHER MOTIVATE EVERY STUDENT?

Like many teachers, I have seen a lot of movies about teachers. Many of the movies, especially those "based on a true story," have a similar theme: A smart young teacher goes to a poor, inner-city school, faces a class of recalcitrant students, each one displaying a different attitude problem, and through her (or his) unwavering dedication to the students as people and ideals of education as a whole, leads the class to success. I like these kinds of stories. They inspire me as a teacher, and when I show them to my classes, they inspire the students.

A good example is the classic 1988 *Stand and Deliver*, based on the story of Jaime Escalante, a high school teacher from inner-city Los Angeles. In one of the more moving scenes, Escalante talks to his class of poor, racial minority students about the challenges they face:

"When you go for a job, the person giving you that job will not want to hear your problems; ergo, neither do I. You're going to work harder here than you've ever worked anywhere else. And the only thing I ask from you is *ganas*: desire. And maybe a haircut. If you don't have the *ganas*, I will give it to you because I'm an expert."

And he does give them the desire. He goads them, urges them, threatens them, praises them, rewards them, yells at them… and he takes them from their failing status in his remedial math class to passing the notoriously difficult AP Calculus exam. (Any student who has ever taken the TOEFL will cringe in sympathy watching these students take that test.)

It's every teacher's dream, isn't it? To be able to supply motivation. And to some extent, I think we can. Every class is a sort of sales opportunity, and you sell your subject area and even the minute details, such as the importance of distinguishing count and non-count nouns.

How responsible are we, though, for every student's motivational level? We might see them for 90 minutes a week, or three hours a week, or in some rare intensive class, even 10 hours a week. That's still a small slice out of a student's life that encompasses work, family, friends, hobbies, romance, and much else that we cannot affect. Sometimes—just sometimes—what we teach in English class is NOT the most important thing going on in their lives, and we need to accept that. Motivation can also be affected by a student's character, personality, and state of mental and physical health. That's a lot for one English teacher to cope with.

To the extent that it's possible, we should of course motivate students as individuals and the class as a group. I don't think it's possible to list techniques that "work" for motivating others because it depends too much on the personality of the individual teacher as well as on the specific class and students in question. However, I do think that the teacher's overall level of enthusiasm for her subject and class is infectious—and that is something that every teacher can work on.

When you fly, there's no more chilling moment for a parent than when you hear that announcement that in the event of an unexpected loss of cabin pressure, you are to secure your own oxygen mask before assisting your children. Anyone can understand the wisdom of that, but you know in your heart how tremendously difficult it would be to not help your child (or, really, anybody's child) first. It's a similar situation with our classes. Our energy level affects the students.

I would argue then that one very good way to motivate your students is to ensure that you do not assign homework faster than you can grade it; that you get around eight hours of sleep a night; that you use your weekends as work-free periods; that you eat protein with your breakfast every day; that you exercise regularly. These are areas of someone's life that you do have control over, because it's your life. When your life is running smoothly, you'll be more likely to have the energy and enthusiasm to lead, cajole, or prod your students into finding their desire.

Finally, I'd like to recommend a different sort of movie about teaching, *The Emperor's Club,* based on the short story "The Palace Thief" (Ethan Canin). Truthfully, I don't know if this was a popular movie or not—I never heard of it in theaters in the US and have never seen any reviews, but I watched it on three different airplane trips, sometimes more than once, so I came to know it well. Mr. Hundert, the teacher, works in an expensive private preparatory school, teaching a class of motivated, hard-working students. Enter a new student, Sedgewick Bell, a poor-little-rich-boy type of much promise and intellect, but no motivation, and of course the requisite poor attitude.

I'll throw in a bit of a spoiler, because what's important about the movie is not the plot line, but the more subtle dynamics of personality.

Hundert tries everything he can to motivate this student—at the expense, however, of a more deserving but less flashy student who does not present himself as "troubled." The top three students in the class every year participate in a trivia competition. Bell, in a late-term burst of sincere effort, came in fourth, so he doesn't qualify. In a scene I think every teacher can relate to, feeling both compassionate and horrified, Hundert changes Bell's score by marking an essay higher, thus qualifying Bell for the contest—and of course disqualifying the student who really did place third. You know why he did it—to motivate Bell and turn his life around and make him love education. And... it doesn't work.

The troubled rich kid succeeds in life—but *not* in the right kind of motivation nor in appreciation for education. Hundert is left for years to question his decision of spending a disproportionate amount of energy on this one student, and on the effects of passing over the quiet boy who did everything he should have and was unfairly excluded from what he earned. Could Bell have been reached in another way? Is it actually possible to reach every student? What students are pushed aside when you reach out to the most glamorous troublemaker? Those are good questions for both a teacher and a class to discuss.

Food for thought: Have you had any "glamorous troublemakers" in class before? How did you handle them? How do you ensure you give attention to students who are already motived as well as to students who are not motivated? Have you had any past successes or failures motivating students?

6

SHOULD LEARNING ENGLISH BE FUN?

It's a hard question, isn't it? Saying *Yes* might imply your classes aren't serious or useful; but who wants to be teacher who says *No*? That's not going to be a popular answer with your classes (or perhaps even your colleagues or your boss). It's not really a yes/no question, though; maybe it would be better expressed as *How much fun should*

learning English be? A better question, but no easier to answer—can you give a number?

What is the question, really? The one question you should be asking about learning, and by extension, your teaching? To me, it's *Why are my students learning English?* Although there are many different answers, depending on the students, I am going to guess that the answer most of them would give, were we to ask this directly, would not be *To have fun.*

My high school-aged son is in his second year of learning Japanese in an American high school. I heard him exclaim, one evening, that he really liked his Japanese textbook. Since I write language learning textbooks, I naturally wanted to know why, and to take a look at his book.

It's frankly not a very exciting textbook, at least visually. It looks like ELT books from 20 or 30 years ago. Black and white, with no photographs. The line drawings are simple and are only used for exercises, not as decoration. The exercises are pretty straightforward—here's a model, here are some substitutions, now get in pairs and do it over and over again. There are no celebrities and no references to current TV shows or movies. There are no crossword puzzles.

I asked my son what he particularly liked about his book, and he said, "It's easy to find the vocabulary in the unit—it's all in a list." Was that the most exciting feature? I asked, and he said yes it was, because that made it easy to study for tests. Were the dialogues exciting? He had no opinion. Did he wish there were color pictures? No opinion. Did he find the exercises fun? "Who cares?" was his answer. I explained that when I wrote textbooks, I was repeatedly asked to design exercises that were fresh yet relevant to students' lives, that presented the material in engaging ways—that were, in a sense, "fun." He laughed at me. "Mom, when I want to have fun, I play the XBOX, or hang out with my friends. I don't study Japanese. What I want is a book that explains things clearly so I can study as efficiently as possible, because I don't have a lot of time. I just want to know the stuff and get a good grade." When pressed, he did say that he would be happy to learn Japanese from a modern attractive textbook with fresh engaging topics—but only as long as he could learn it as well and as quickly as he could do it with his current book.

To put it another way: You're turning 11 years old. For your birthday party, would you rather have a party with pony rides and a clown who can fold balloons into whimsical shapes, or would you rather have an ESL teacher come and give a rousing lesson on the present perfect? If you're an adult, would you rather go to a jazz club with your friends, or have a little study group that examines the way transitions are used to connect paragraphs in an essay? How about learning the proper way to cite sources using APA formatting? No? Our students, for the most part, are not trying to have "fun" in class. They're trying to learn English.

Now, certainly there are some students who are learning English because of a strong affinity for literature, who will go on to become poets and craftspeople who work with English because of a pure love of the language. However, I think most students want English to do well in school, or get a job, or travel, or interact with other people with whom English would be the common language; and for those students, what is going to make them happiest is **success**. Knowing the language. The extent to which an enjoyable activity leads them to this success is what should drive our choice to use this activity, and not whether the activity is a fun game in and of itself. Fun in the classroom now with no appreciable achievement in their learning goals will give you a class of students that laughs happily in every class and is ultimately unhappy and angry and the end of the term—and rightfully so. Activities that might seem repetitious or mundane, if they result in students learning the language, are actually going to please them more.

As stated before, though, "Should learning English be fun?" is not a yes/no question. It's not that simple. Of course if you can assist students in their goal of learning the language quickly and thoroughly, and you can do so in an enjoyable way, you should by all means do so! There is only a problem when those two goals conflict, and a teacher choose enjoyable over useful.

The question, therefore, that you should be asking yourself when selecting textbooks and exercises and games, when designing your own activities and worksheets, is not *Is this a fun activity?* but *How is this going to help my students learn English?* Once you are sure that the activity is worthwhile in the sense of being practical, then you can refine it or spice it up or dress it up as a game. Go ahead and be entertaining—once you are sure that you are meeting the needs of students as learners of the language. Ensure that your classes are useful and efficient, and your students will be grateful and, yes, happy.

Food for thought: Think about your current or recent students. Why are they (or were they) learning English? What steps do you take to help them see their own progress? Think of an activity you do in class that is fun. How does it also help students improve their English? When you do this activity, do you make its usefulness explicit to your students?

7

MODELING STUDENT TALK

How can I get students to talk more? is a question I frequently get, especially in parts of the world known for quieter classrooms. Now, I don't always want students to talk more. Sometimes, I want them to listen, or to summarize briefly, or to respond in writing. However, I do want them to make the most of their talking time; in essence, to talk better.

These days, many textbooks are set up to give students "communicative tasks," where they speak English to exchange information. Often, there is some sort of deed to be done—A has the information that B needs, and B has the information that A needs, and they speak to exchange their information and fill in their charts or solve the puzzle or whatever end goal there is.

Those can be enjoyable tasks, but the downside of overdoing them is that students get used to seeing every speaking task as a sort of info gap: That is, there is information that must be exchanged, and so once it is exchanged, the task is over. It's a fine method for completing one's "Find Someone Who" worksheet, but it fails miserably for a discussion. Discussion questions look like they're asking for information (that is, students' opinions on a topic, or answers to some questions), but so much more goes on in a good discussion. Participants might make or respond to jokes, show off, show understanding or sympathy, address new topics, search for new vocabulary, let off steam, learn and teach information about the topic, express frustration, and so on.

I remember one lesson in particular with a small group of trainees at Sumitomo Electric Industries (SEI) whom I'd had in class for about six months. They had a good command of vocabulary and grammar, they were lively and engaged, and of course they were happy to be in English class instead of back at their desks.

We had a unit in the textbook on receiving visitors,

leading up to office and factory tours; quite relevant for these trainees, since they used English primarily for receiving overseas visitors and then showing them around. There was vocabulary to be learned and dialogues to practice and functions to employ, but first there were (as there often are in textbooks) some warm-up questions. In my mind, they'd spend about 15 minutes on these warm-up questions (though I was prepared to go longer), during which they'd bring up the necessary vocabulary that they knew, as well as signal to me what they didn't know. Also, I'd get a feel for their past experiences and needs.

There were two questions, more or less like this:

1. Have you ever received a visitor at your company? Who?
2. Where did you meet him or her?

As it turned out that day, I had four trainees in class, so I put them in pairs. And in each pair, the "discussion" went like this:

A: Ah ... B-san, "Have you ever received a visitor at your company? Who?"
B: Ah ... yes. Sato-san.
A: OK. "Where did you meet him or her?"
B: At ... Kansai Kuukou.
A: Airport.
B: Airport. OK, switch! A-san, "Have you ever received a visitor at your company? Who?"
A: No.
B: "Where did you..." *Ah, so ka.* "No." (*both laugh*)

They looked at me expectantly. Time for the listening! Epic fail, as the gamers would say. I sighed. The students were perplexed. They asked if they'd done something wrong.

"It wasn't what I was expecting," I said.

A nodded in understanding. " 'No, I haven't,' right?"

No, I said, it wasn't the grammar, it was the information. True confusion now. "But ... I only met Sato," said B, a bit apologetically. And I laughed. Naturally, they wanted to know what was so funny. Well, we had time, so I thought, why not talk about it?

"What is the purpose of these questions?" I asked.

They had the look of students expecting some sort of trick. "To know what visitors we met?" asked A.

No! Here was our problem. I explained that I actually didn't care how many people they'd met, or who, or where. The purpose of the questions was to bring up vocabulary and functions and grammar necessary to talk about receiving visitors, and to talk about issues concerning visitors, particularly international visitors, and to practice meeting visitors in English over and over again until they could do it comfortably on their own.

Then, I modeled what I had been hoping for. I went over and sat with the students and role-played the discussion myself, taking the part of both students, like this:

A: Hi, B-san. Receiving visitors. I don't have much experience with that topic.
B: Really? I do.
A: Oh? Have you ever received any visitors?

B: Yes, only one time. But I think I'll meet more in the future, because it's part of my job now.
A: Who did you meet?
B: Mr. Sato from the Head Office.
A: Did you already know him?
B: A little. I hadn't met him before, but I speak to him on the phone almost every week.
A: How did you know who he was, then? Did you make a sign with his name?
B: No, I knew his picture from (*checks with imaginary teacher for vocabulary help, and gets it*) the Intranet.
A: Did he look like his picture?
B: Actually, not really. His hair was longer. But you know, he was carrying a blue SEI shopping bag. So I knew it was him.

And so on. The students looked amazed. Truly. They'd had no idea, no idea at all, that this was what I might want; just as I'd had no idea that they didn't know. They weren't being uncooperative; they didn't lack vocabulary or grammar or energy; they weren't bored. They just didn't know what my expectations were, or even what the purpose of the exercise was. Once they knew what to do, they put the books down and had a good 20-minute discussion on the topic, and ended energized for the rest of the lesson.

I'm a huge modeler now, and I don't wait for things to go wrong first. Whether I want brief, focused answers or a meandering discussion, I never want to turn students loose on a task if they don't know what its purpose is or how to do it.

Food for thought: How often do you provide models of 'freer' activities such as discussions or writing assignments? If you ever get less-than-wonderful results from these activities, do you think modeling could help? How could you introduce some models?

8

TEACHING PRE-READING SKILLS

Some years ago I spent two weeks in Libya at Al Fatah University working with final year graduate students who would become English teachers; and who actually already were English teachers, working as Teaching Assistants in the English department. I decided to spend one lesson each on speaking, vocabulary, writing, reading, and grammar. We'd spend the first part of the lesson working on the skills themselves, I figured, and the second part of the lesson talking about how to teach that skill.

When we got to the reading lesson, I asked the prospective teachers if they thought there were such things as "reading strategies." In my experiences with SE Asian students, I've noticed that often students think reading means nothing more than decoding words and then learning a ton of vocabulary. The Libyans knew a lot of the right answers—skimming, scanning, reading for main ideas, reading for details, making inferences; and they could trot definitions of these right out.

As practice, I gave them a chapter of a reading book I'd recently written, *Building Academic Reading Skills 1* (University of Michigan Press). The level of the readings themselves were below these students' proficiency level, so I assumed they'd have no trouble applying the strategies.

Wrong! Each reading (two per chapter) in the book begins (after some warm-up questions for the topic) with a Predict, a Skim, and a Scan exercise. But, as soon as they started with the first Predict question, which directed them to look at the title, they started reading intensively. I stopped them, and in a few cases had to ask them to turn their papers over. The skimming and scanning were even harder. I watched one student, who had in fact provided me with the very correct definitions of skimming and scanning when I'd asked, actually pick up his pen and start moving it along under each word, underlining some, circling others. "Ahmed," I said (not his real name), "you're reading every word, aren't you?" He looked stricken. "Yes, but I can't help it! I just *must* read everything!"

We stopped the class and talked about what was happening. I recognize that I was extraordinarily fortunate to have students whose listening and speaking levels, as well as their reflective abilities, were high enough that they could talk about what was going on in their heads.

Ahmed, as it turned out, was a literature aficionado; and normally one doesn't skim or scan a novel or short story. However, these students were also struggling with the reading section of the TOEFL and with their own academic reading for their graduate school courses. We had a nice discussion about different types of reading approaches for different types of texts, and since every student in the class admitted to having difficulty getting through the amount of reading they had, understanding the texts, and remembering what they read, they promised to at least try the strategies I was proposing.

On to the next text. This time, they got through the Predict, Skim, and Scan exercises without reading intensively (though I admit to standing behind Ahmed and whacking him lightly on the shoulders with a bat whenever I thought he was succumbing) (that is, a rubber toy model of the animal, not a piece of sports equipment; our readings were both on bats).

Now came the moment I both anticipate and dread as a teacher—when I've recommended something that I'm 85% sure will work for the students, but can't in my heart quite guarantee. But, oh, happy day! Yes, after students read intensively and did the exercises, they all said that they had found that the intensive reading went faster and that the exercises were easier to do (and yes, I knew from previous classes that if they had not found a strategy useful, they would have happily said so). Ahmed in fact stopped by my office later and asked for more short texts to practice these strategies on.

Pre-reading strategies are a bit like the first two steps of process writing (brainstorming and organizing), I find—most students see them as steps that take more time; and yet, applied correctly, they actually make the process more efficient. A good reader saves time not just by being able to move through the text more quickly but by being able to understand it and remember it better.

My take-away from this experience is that as teachers we need to explain the purpose of reading strategies and not just teach how to apply them; and that further, these explanations need to be repeated, re-affirmed, and re-proven. In addition, students need opportunities to practice the strategies over and over again. It's not enough to skim in Chapter 2, scan in Chapter 3, and find some details in Chapter 4. When I wrote the next level in the *Building Academic Reading Skills* series, then, I made sure that I had students apply the strategies over and over and over again, and that I provided frequent short explanations of the intention and value of these strategies.

Whatever textbook you use for teaching reading, or if you select your own texts, I recommend a similar approach: practice the skills that you've taught over and over, with each text. Don't assume that because students have (for example) scanned once, they'll automatically scan every new reading from now on. Skimming and scanning and making inferences and so on are skills, and skills take practice. Students will see an improvement in their reading ability over time, as they apply the skills again and again.

> **Food for thought:** How many of the reading passages in the textbooks you currently use have skimming and scanning exercises for every reading? For those readings that don't include these skills, could you add them?

9

ADVICE TO A YOUNG IRANIAN ENGLISH TEACHER

AzarGrammar.com, a website I wrote many of the essays in this book for (but which sadly no longer exists) received a letter from a young English teacher in Iran who asked for advice on how to continue his English and teaching studies in a native English-speaking country such as the US. Below is my response to him (the name has been changed). **Note from 2022:** This letter was written in 2018. I wish I could say the political situation has changed, but unfortunately, it has not. However, the advice is not country-specific; I would say the same thing to any English teacher who wished to travel to an English-speaking country but could not.

∼

Dear Ibrahim,

This letter is in response to your email to the AzarGrammar.com site that asks about studying abroad, particularly in the US, to become a better English teacher.

There are two main styles of writing in American English: One that starts at the beginning and works logically towards the end, and one that starts with the conclusion and then fills in the background explanation. This answer will follow the latter style.

No, I'm sorry to say, I don't have any good advice for you on how to get to the US. Even if the entire question of finances—air ticket, rent for an apartment, food, utilities, books, tuition, and so on—were not an issue, a visa is. This is not an easy time for people from your country to travel to mine, any more than it is for people from my country to travel to yours. In particular, it is difficult, if not downright impossible, for young, single men from many countries to get non-immigrant visas to the US. It's beyond the scope of this letter for me to argue whether that is right or wrong, although I will say that I remember to this day the frustration I felt when my fiancé was not allowed into the

US on a tourist visa so that we could marry here (instead, we married abroad).

At the same time, though, I do have a more hopeful answer for you, which is that it absolutely is possible to be an excellent user of English and an excellent teacher of English without ever visiting the US or England or any other native English-speaking country. Two of my favorite authors, Joseph Conrad from Poland and Ved Mehta from India, learned English as adults, and largely before they ever visited another country at all.

I've personally met enthusiastic and talented groups of teachers in countries such as Ukraine, Libya, Algeria, and Yemen who had excellent English language skills, as well as excellent teaching skills, who had never left their own country before or met a native speaker of English before me. As a non-native speaker, in fact, you are a powerful and inspiring model for your students. Some of my best editors of ELT textbooks have been non-native speakers.

Developing strong English and teaching skills is easier than it has ever been, thanks to improved mail services and, of course, the Internet, which makes it possible not only to read and write in English but to listen extensively to radio shows, news programs, and songs. Groups of English teachers communicate all over the world through social media. You can read articles about the English language and about specific classroom teaching issues. You can ask questions of other teachers and answer their questions, discuss topics, and share classroom stories and teaching techniques. You can download free resources to use in class. You can match your students to keypals or more traditional penpals in other countries so that they can practice their English as well. You can find individual teachers with whom you feel a personal connection and develop an email relationship. You can follow YouTube, Instagram, and TikTok teachers and use their videos in class.

Actually, it turns out that I'm going to use a blended genre here for the organization of my letter. While I started with an answer to your question, I'm going to end with a more important conclusion.

As I noted, this is not an easy time between our two countries; and in fact, it's not an easy time for many countries in the world. Now, more than ever before, it's crucial for people to study languages other than their own. Would Americans be less afraid of Iranians if more of us studied Farsi in school? I believe so. Language is an essential clue to how people think and experience the world and express their thoughts and emotions. It's not a question of adapting to another culture, or being overcome by a different system, but of understanding other ways.

I know it's frustrating to sit in your home or your classroom and feel overwhelmed by world events that it seems you can't control or even question. However, I really believe that there is nothing better that you, Ibrahim, can do to promote world peace than to teach your classes with sincerity and love. You could do this in a math, science, or history class too, but language touches on our contemporary world and lives in such deep and wide ways that I think you will have even more impact in this way.

You have a tremendous power to affect and change lives. Please see each obstacle that you face as a challenge and not a barrier. And welcome to the world of language teachers. We are so glad to have you!

Best wishes,

Dorothy Zemach

Food for thought: Do you believe it's important for an English teacher to visit an English-speaking country? Why or why not? What are some ways that English teachers around the world can connect with others to improve both their own English levels and their teaching skills?

10

ELEVATOR PITCH

I take an aerobics class several times a week. The same people tend to show up at the same class times, and after a while, we get a little friendly, although locker room chitchat tends to revolve around exercise or the weather. However, recently, one of the women I talk to revealed that she is a high school biology teacher. That prompted me to mention that I work in education as well, in ESL. She said, "Oh, I have a number of international students in my classes. I have to go soon, but... what is one thing you could tell me about international students that you think I should know?"

Oh, my. It's a big question, isn't it? There is so much more to tell than just one thing! And yet... she's out the door, and she doesn't have time for me to cram my career and my degree into her head. She really does just want, at the moment, to know one thing. One thing that might make a difference, that isn't too hard to understand, that can be communicated quickly.

Here's the one thing I chose to tell her: That some of the mistakes that students make in writing that look like very simple things—mistakes with a, the, and choice of prepositions—are actually very high-level mistakes. They do not (necessarily) indicate a poor command of English, and cannot be cleared up in a few hours of study.

She knew exactly what I was talking about, and also said (since I asked) that they didn't really obscure meaning, just made her wonder about the writers' English ability. She asked what the solution was, and I said, to have those students make an American friend that they could treat to a coffee or a milkshake in return for some simple proofreading—because those are very easy mistakes for a native speaker to catch and correct, even a high school student with no ESL background.

As a parting remark, I said she should tell her international students that receiving such help was not "cheating." She assured me she didn't thing it was dishonest; but the important thing, I felt, was to make sure

49

that her students knew that, since if they're from another culture they might not have any idea whether she did or not, and penalties in American high schools for cheating can be severe.

She thanked me for my advice, which she said she found very helpful, and the next time we ran into each other I think we talked about sore thigh muscles (that particular exercise instructor is very fond of "walking lunges"). I suppose if she has specific questions in the future, and crosses my path again, she might ask for more advice, but for the moment, she had what she needed.

Are you familiar with the concept of the "elevator pitch"? It's a term used by aspiring writers, the idea that you should be able to quickly summarize the plot of your novel to an agent in the time it takes you both to ride the elevator to wherever you're going. Times give for an elevator pitch are around 30 second to up to two minutes. They're brief.

It occurs to me that we have many chances in our lives to give elevator pitches for our field of knowledge and our careers. You're at a party, and someone asks you what you do. "I teach English as a second language," you say, and they respond with "What does that mean?" (or the one I usually get, "Wow, you must speak a lot of other languages!"). What would you say about ESL to someone unfamiliar with it, if you only had two minutes?

What would you say about teaching? How about in response to "That must be an easy job—you go home at 3:00 and you get your summers off!"?

I think it's worth thinking about our elevator pitches in advance, before we're put on the spot. So I invite readers of this column to take the time now to think of what one idea —not even the most important idea, just one that is important at all, and/or interesting—would you want to say about English or teaching or ESL or materials writing or whatever you, if you had two minutes in which to say it?

Food for thought: The questions are all in the article! But here's another one. What would you say —briefly!—to someone who said, "Anybody who speaks English can be an English teacher"?

11
MAY I HAVE A COPY OF YOUR PRESENTATION?

Ah, conference season! These days, of course, it's really year-round, as different countries have their regional and national conferences at different times. For about the past decade, it's become common for conferences to ask presenters if they'd like to have their emails printed in the program book. I always say yes, because one reason I attend conferences is to make connections with other professionals.

This is the first year, though, that I've had a slew of emails post-conference, from people I don't remember meeting, requesting that I send them my entire presentation.

Some, of course, are not legitimate—like the one that began "Dear Sir or Madam" and was apparently sent to every email address in the TESOL program book, even to people who hadn't given a presentation. But others are genuine; often from teachers who didn't attend the presentation.

I have mixed feelings about this. On the one hand, I am sympathetic to teachers who had to miss one presentation because they were attending another (or were giving their own). I am sympathetic too to teachers who couldn't stay for the whole conference, or who perhaps couldn't attend at all, because of work or family commitments, or lack of financial support.

Overall, though, I'm not comfortable sending out my presentations to people who did not originally attend them. There are a few reasons.

The most important is that I don't think my presentations would make much sense from just the slides. Most of a typical talk for me is just that—talking. It's not written down, although there are brief notes on some slides. I worry that a picture would simply make no sense without me there to explain it. For example, what point am I making with these slides from the same recent talk? Different people would have different guesses, and probably nobody would get the points I made with these images without hearing what I had to say about them.

∼

Photo credit: Scott Rhea

In another recent talk, promoting a new coursebook series, I have one slide (not from the series!) that's an example of a *bad* dialogue. Suppose that presentation goes out into the wide world, tied to my name, and somehow people assume that it's supposed to be an example of a *good* dialogue? How will someone who wants to give my presentation (as several emails have said they wish to do) be able to answer questions that follow?

Finally, the presentations that I put together represent a lot of time and work. I spend time considering what to say and writing an outline; I spend time choosing images and designing the presentation to be visually engaging. Often the information that I'm presenting is the result of years of work or study, and the conclusions are my original thoughts. I'm proud of the presentations I give; they represent an important part of my professional life. At the risk of sounding arrogant (sorry!), I consider the presentations I give to be a reward for those people who attended the conference (who often pay to attend, and at the very least give up some of their precious time and energy).

Now, I do have sympathy for people who wish to listen to a presentation but not take copious notes; and I would rather have people paying attention and listening than trying to take photos of every slide. For those people—who have attended the presentation—I'm happy to make a .pdf version of some of the slides available. In these cases, though, I modify the presentation somewhat, and remove some slides of images that would make no sense on their own, although I leave in those that would trigger the memory of anyone who already saw the presentation.

In these days of webinars and online presentations, a related issue that comes up is whether that presentation should be made available to the world via YouTube or a similar streaming platform. I have on occasion given my permission for videos of talks I've done to remain on YouTube (my IATEFL plenary on ELT materials, for instance, is here: https://www.youtube.com/watch?v=xI-OLoBxENI&t=2163s). But often I'm paid for my online presentations, and I tailor them to a specific audience—and then no, I don't want them available for free on YouTube, or I'd never be able to use that material again. It's been suggested to me that I record my favorite talks and then sell them on my own somehow, but I'm not comfortable with that either. Mostly, then, I ask that recordings of my talks be only made available, in a closed system, to people who attended the conference or event.

I feel I am a pretty accessible person. I have a Facebook page that is open to any teachers who are interested in talking about language teaching and learning, and I answer questions about my textbooks and thoughts on the ELT profession. I'm on LinkedIn and Instagram. I present worldwide. I am thrilled that technology has removed so many barriers—geographical, time, and financial—to worldwide discussions in our profession. Given all that, I hope teachers can understand why I don't feel comfortable emailing my conference presentations.

Food for thought: Do you send out your presentations post-conference? Why or why not? How do you feel about presentations you've given being posted on YouTube?

12

A SICK POLICY?

I recently subbed three ESL classes for a friend at a large US university. She'd known of her upcoming absence for at least a week, and left lesson plans and notes for me, and all necessary photocopies and papers. All I had to do was appear and conduct her lessons. I was paid for my time by the university.

However, the experience reminded me of just how unusual it was, at least at university programs in the US. Normally, at this university (as has been my experience at all of the other American universities where I have taught), an absent teacher is expected to arrange for a colleague to sub the class, free of charge—or to pay the sub out of his/her own pocket. Additionally, one is expected to prepare a lesson plan and materials—which of course is harder to do if one is sick. For this reason, many teachers—even those who have sick leave, which not all of them do—actually find it less stressful to teach while sick. I've known teachers with complete laryngitis who taught their lessons entirely through mime and writing, rather than miss one lesson.

Interestingly, this system of having every class subbed by someone seems to be somewhat unique to ESL. In other departments, if a professor is sick, the department secretary hangs a note to that effect on the classroom door, and class is canceled. Students don't seem to mind all that much, either—it's like a personal snow day. Work is made up in the next class session or electronically through email or programs such as Blackboard.

I remember once teaching French classes at a university, and I had to miss the Wednesday before Thanksgiving for a professional conference. I asked every French teacher I could find to substitute for me, but they were all teaching at the same time. When I met with the Department Chair to explain my problem, he was nonplussed. First he asked me why I thought any students were going to show up in the afternoon before a holiday weekend (something I hadn't even considered), and then asked me why I didn't just cancel the classes. "But I won't be able to make them up later," I explained. His response was, "So?" And so I canceled the classes, and no, it didn't seem to through my semester into turmoil.

I've never known an ESL class to be canceled like that, however. Somehow, a sub is always found. I've worked at American universities where teachers were explicitly told when hired that they should find a "friend" on the faculty with whom they would agree to sub for.

The problem is, of course, that not everyone is absent the same number of days each term. Some people get sick more often than others, or need time off every now and then to care for sick family members—which meant that some people wound up subbing a lot more often than their colleagues, which led to hard feelings. Additionally, as was the case in the French department, many classes are held at the same times, so that one can't necessarily sub for a friend even if one wants to. And finally, the stress of preparing a lesson plan that someone else can pick up and follow is sometimes too much to cope with when one is already feeling sick enough to be considering missing a class. The solution that has been sometimes presented to me is to always have an "emergency lesson plan" at the ready, that someone could come in and teach at any point in the term—but I probably don't need to explain here that such a thing is not always possible for every class.

Now, I do see the other side of the issue too. Students have paid money to attend a class, and have the right to expect that class will be held. It's hard enough to cover all of one's material in a term when everything runs smoothly; missing hours of instruction time just makes it harder. If I really thought that one of my lessons wasn't necessary or important, then I wouldn't have done my job as a teacher in preparing it. Still, though, I can't subscribe to the notion that the whole system will come crashing down upon us if a class is canceled every now and then—and I do think there's a real harm being done to teachers who feel pressured into teaching while sick (not to mention a harm to those around them).

I can't, from here, recommend a system that will work for every institution. I know that the best system I ever encountered was at the American Language Center in Rabat, Morocco: If a teacher was sick, he/she called in and said so. A lesson plan for the sub was appreciated, but not required (a detailed curriculum existed for each class, so a sub could walk in and know reasonably well what should be covered that day). Teachers were not allowed to arrange for their own substitutes (to avoid pressure on one's friends). Instead, the Center arranged for a sub—and, the Center paid subs at 1.5 their regular rate, so subbing was actually something that a lot of people were happy to take on. So that is my model for an ideal situation, in case any program administrators are reading this blog. Let's remember that in many universities, there is no requirement that ESL teachers alone among the faculty find subs and remunerate them out of their own pocket; it's a custom that somehow we have all chosen, and therefore, we have the power to alter it.

What I can recommend, strongly, is that every teacher interviewing for a job ask about the institution's policy on absences; and for all currently employed teachers to think about what they would do if they had to miss a class. Is it possible to have an "anyone can do it at any time" lesson plan in reserve? Is it time to create a more detailed syllabus, just in case some day someone needed to walk into your class cold? Do you have a friend who could sub for you? Are you willing and able to sub for others? What are your personal thoughts on teaching while sick, and do your students and colleagues share those convictions? What are your legal rights?

And finally... a reminder to others as well as myself that good diet, frequent exercise, and adequate sleep reduce our chances of becoming ill in the first place.

Food for thought: What do you do about your classes if you're sick? What is your institution's stated policy? How do you feel about other people teaching your class? How do you feel about teaching someone else's class—would you need a detailed lesson plan in advance? What are your most effective ways of ensuring you stay as healthy as possible?

13

SHOULD STUDENTS USE A GRAMMAR CHECKER?

I'm old enough to have learned to type on a typewriter, not a word processor. Personal computers arrived as I was leaving college; I got my first Macintosh my senior year. Oh, the glory! Saving! Cutting and pasting! Spellcheck! Wonderful tools.

Of course, like all wonderful tools, these need to be

used with some care; and there are other tools available to writers that are not wonderful at all.

A spellchecker is a writer's friend. It catches your typing mistakes as well as the mistakes you make because you honestly don't know how to spell a word. It can't catch everything – if you mean you're but write your, the mistake will not be fixed. To find that kind of mistake, you still need a good understanding of English, and to reread your papers carefully to make sure you wrote what you meant.

Still, though, spellcheckers catch a lot. I advise students to spellcheck every paper before turning it in; I also advise them to spellcheck emails sent to professors, staff, supervisors, coworkers, clients – in short, anyone with whom they have a formal relationship.

The grammar checker, though ... ah, that is another story. It would be wonderful, I know, to have an automated way to fix your grammar, or even just to point out where things were wrong. And who knows, maybe someday we'll get one. But we don't have it yet. The grammar checker is one tool I advise students not to use. Ever. And I'm going to show you why.

The examples in this article, all screen shots from my grammar checker, come from novels written by Russell Blake, a well-known writer of thrillers, mysteries, and suspense novels. He's a native English speaker and a good writer. Like most professional writers, after carefully checking his own work (he does three complete drafts on his own), he sends the manuscript to an editor (me).

I do some light fact-checking (if a man runs into the subway in Prague at 4:00 am to escape an assassin, I check to make sure that the subway is open and running then), I watch for words used too often, I make sure the love interest's eye color doesn't change between chapters, I make sure phrases in a foreign language and international place names are spelled correctly. And I check his grammar, for both accuracy and variety.

You might be wondering why, if I think the grammar checker is so bad, I use it myself. Well, one thing it does catch is extra spaces between words or sentences. While these aren't so noticeable in a term paper, they'll mess up the look of an ebook.

But one thing the grammar checker won't do is correctly is check your grammar.

Here's why. The grammar checker is programmed to check certain things – subject/verb agreement, pronoun use, hyphenation, commonly confused words, and so on. But while those are problematic areas, English is simply too complex for the program to accurately catch mistakes.

In addition, weirdly, it will flag every use of the passive, or at least what it thinks is the passive, and suggest rewording it to the active voice. But there is nothing wrong with the passive used appropriately! Of course, you don't want to use the passive inappropriately, but you don't want to use the active voice inappropriately either. The grammar checker won't help you with that. Instead, it will make the writer feel insecure about perfectly reasonable sentences, and suggest rewordings that are worse. For example:

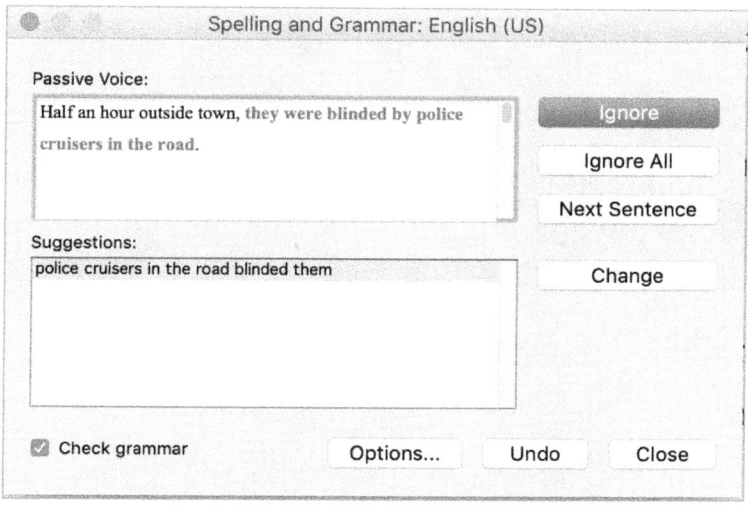

Let's have a look at some the other areas.

Subject-verb agreement is something that many English language learners struggle with; and Word is struggling right along with them.

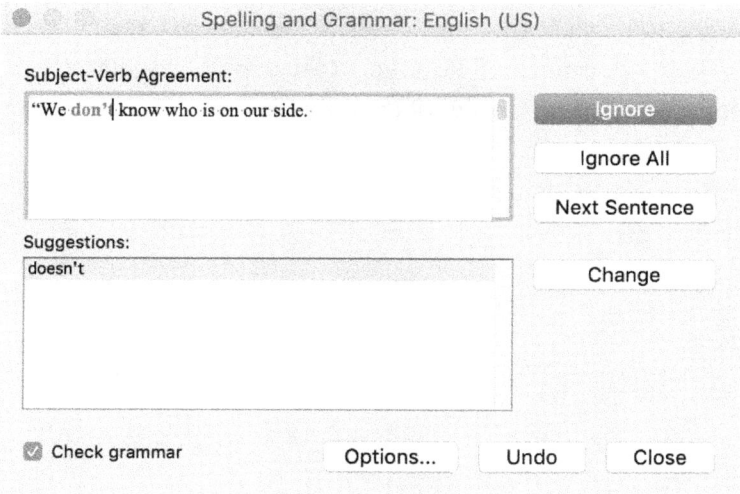

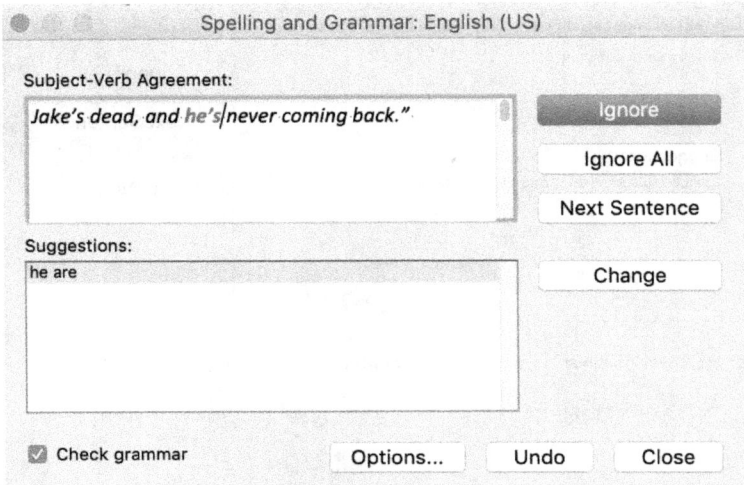

How about pronoun use? Again, we have problems. The grammar checker will for some reason flag every reflexive pronoun and suggest you use an object pronoun. It also tends to suggest that most uses of *them* should really be *his or her*. Regardless of how you feel about 'singular they', sometimes *them* really does refer to several people—or items!

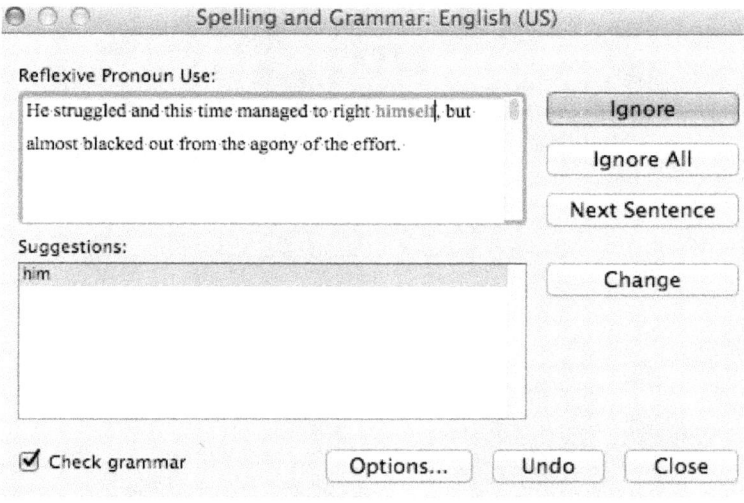

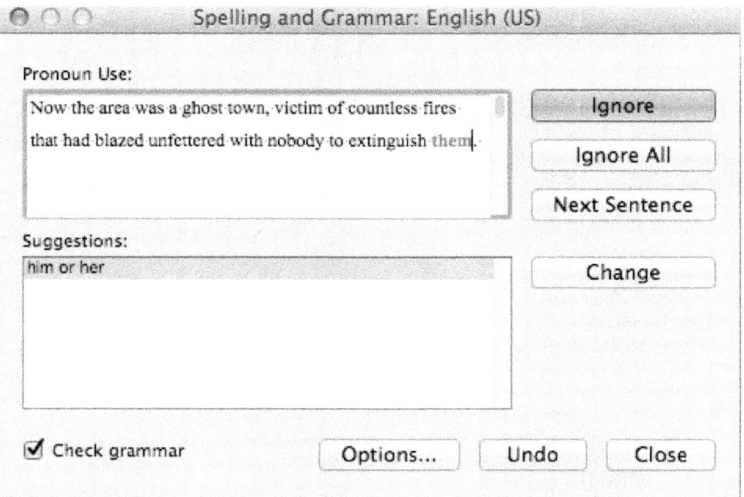

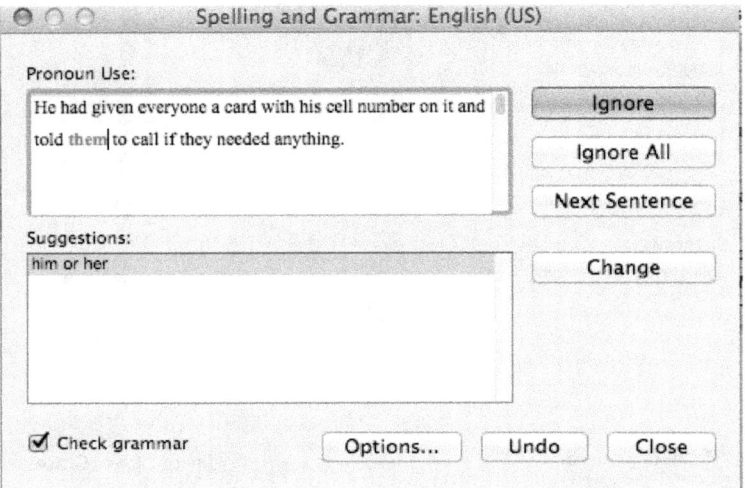

The grammar checker has certain pairs of words programmed into it to flag as commonly confused. Yet it often suggests you change the correct choice to the incorrect choice:

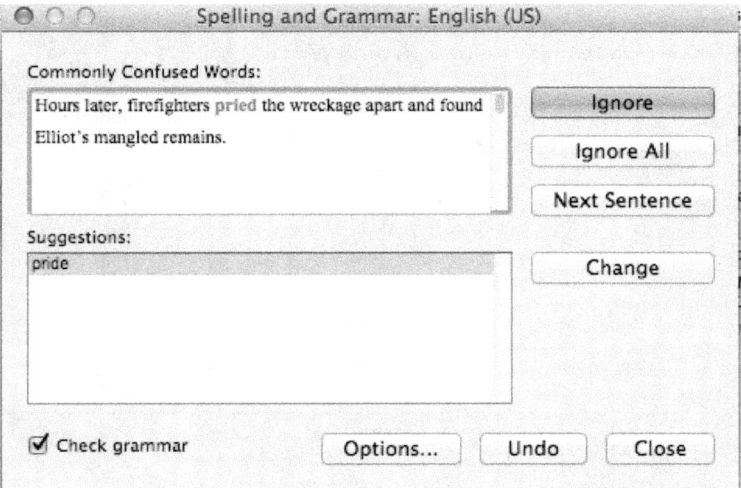

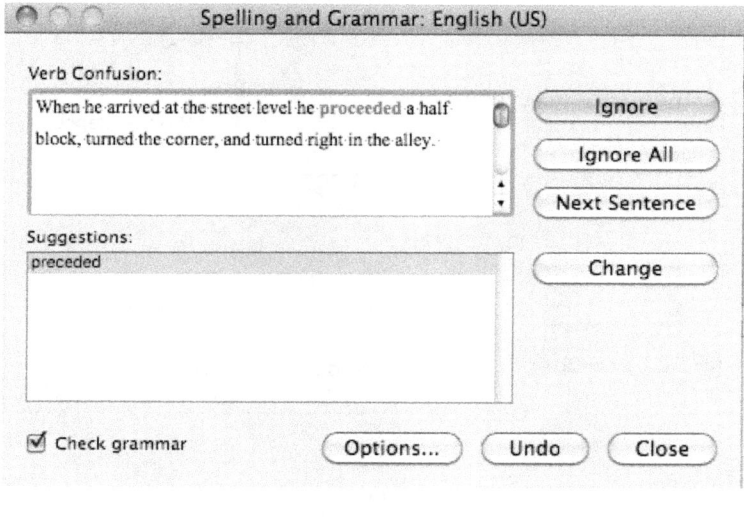

In particular, it struggles with *they're, their,* and *there,* with hilarious results:

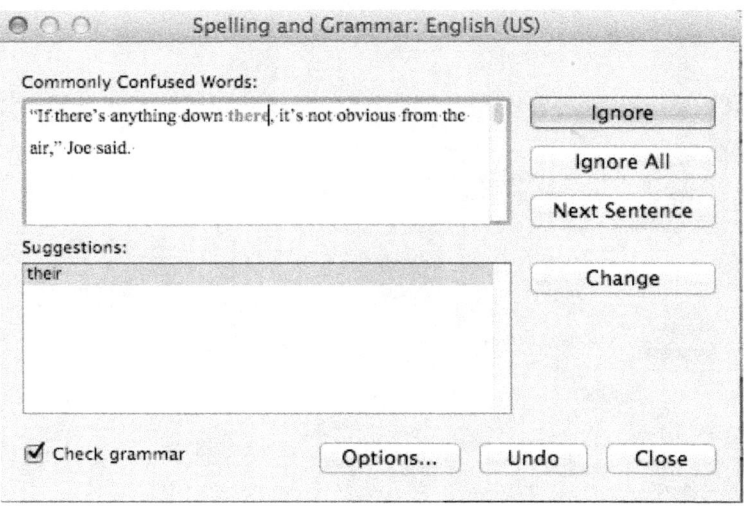

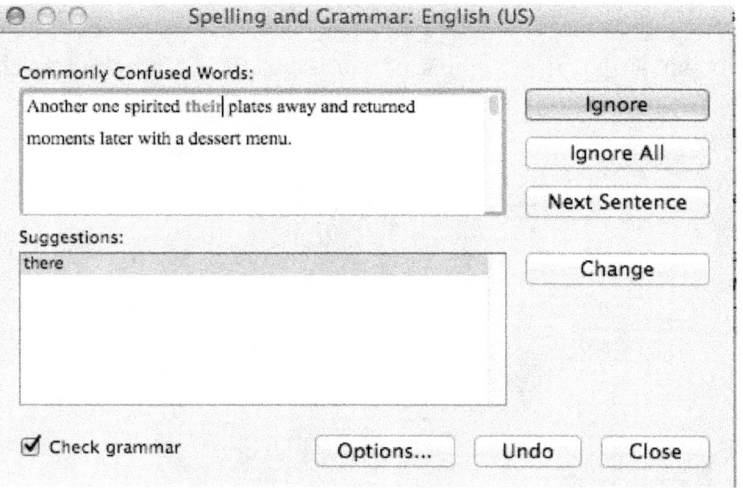

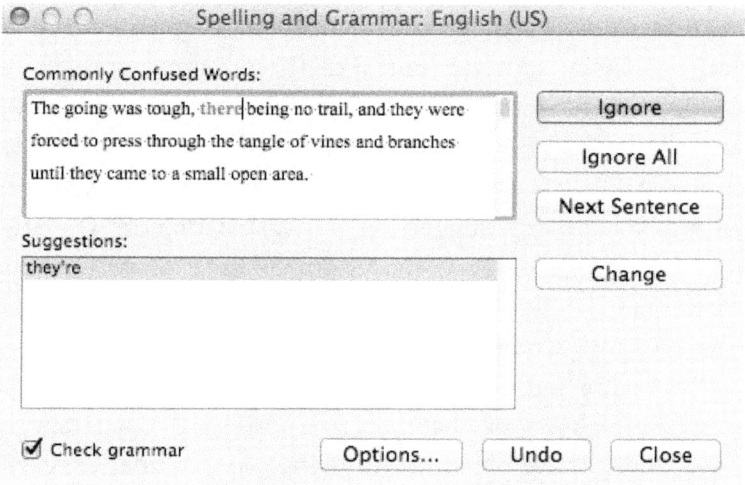

Have a look at the suggestions for rewording here, from what the grammar checked has (incorrectly) identified as a problem with conjunction use:

And so on. If you're already adept at English grammar, you can easily spot the mistakes the grammar checker is making and ignore them. But for someone learning English, it's terribly confusing. The learner can see that the category chosen is indeed problematic; but should the grammar checker's suggestion be trusted or not? For any learner below C1 level, the grammar checker will either slow them down or, worse, guide them into making mistakes they wouldn't have otherwise.

If you're working with students who are word-processing papers or documents or correspondence, talk to them about the problems with using the grammar checker. I recommend that students turn off the feature on Word that checks grammar as they type, for example, because the wiggly green lines underneath parts of the sentence can be very distracting—especially when they're wrong.

Show students some examples from the grammar checker (you're welcome to use the ones in this article) and discuss why what's shown as incorrect really isn't. If you have the time to build a longer lesson, take a student's paper and run it through the grammar checker. Screenshot examples of things both correctly and incorrectly flagged, and then discuss them with the class. If you have a student's permission and the appropriate equipment, you could even do this in class by projecting the paper on a screen and running the grammar check while the class watches. Discuss together everything that it catches.

Students should absolutely check their writing for grammatical errors, and they can make use of peer editing and a teacher's advice, but they can't rely on an automated tool.

Food for thought: Do you expect your students to use a spellchecker? Do you give any explicit instruction on how to best use one? What can you tell students who want to know how to edit their own work for grammatical accuracy?

14

MY DEAR

If Facebook were a country, it would be the largest one on earth (see exact stats from 2018 here https://qz.com/1386649/social-networks-make-the-worlds-largest-nations-seem-small). That's a lot of people… and some days, it feels like most of them are sending me chat messages on Facebook.

Now, there is much that I value about Facebook, and much benefit that I derive from it specifically as an English teacher and textbook writer. That is perhaps a post for another day. Today I want to look specifically at the chat function, and why it causes me so many problems—even with other English teachers. (I should note here that I do accept friend requests from ELT teachers I don't know, because I figure we have a profession in common, and conversations on my main page, which are often about some aspect of English or language or teaching or reading and writing, are richer with more participants.)

For one thing, I find chat in general (not just Facebook's) invasive and demanding. Email I can respond to at my leisure—chat is pressure. I answer, and instantly there's another prompt I have to respond to. Now, if it's important, I don't mind that—in fact, I want that speed and immediacy. I use chat then with people I work with, who need a fast answer to something pressing. I also use it with my son, because that's the fastest way to reach him—although even then, I use it when we need to discuss something urgent. If I'm just checking in, I send a text message.

But with my friends and colleagues, I never use chat to say "Hi, what's up?" And I never, ever use chat to say "Hi, what's up?" to a complete stranger. To me, that's like barging into someone's house without knocking on the door first. You can do that if your car is on fire. But if you don't know me, and you enter my house for no reason without calling in advance and then ringing the doorbell, I'm likely to call the police.

Clearly, that is not how everyone uses Facebook, or I

wouldn't get so many strangers sending me the "Hi" messages. Often, in fact, that is the entire message—"Hi." From someone I don't recognize. I have no idea what sort of response they are expecting. Do they want me to stop in the middle of my work day and respond with "Hi" as well? Do we then move on to "How are you?" and "Fine, thanks, and you"? But why? Why would we (two virtual strangers, with nothing more in common than that we both teach English) do that? Having no good response, I ignore those messages. Sometimes the sender stops; but sometimes the sender keeps messaging me. After five or six, I'll usually write back and ask the person not to. But then that takes a little back and forth for me to explain it, and I feel irritated that I had to spend the time, and uncomfortable because I'm sure I'm being perceived as rude.

As an example, look what happened here.

Stranger: Hi.

Me: Sorry, can I help you with something?
(I am annoyed—I've been interrupted, with no polite phrase or explanation. Still, it could be work related, so I'll ask if he needs help.)

Stranger:
Sorry too
You have Nothing to help me with
As you are not superior to me
We are equal
You can just exchange ideas
That's It

(The stranger is now annoyed too. He is, as it will turn out, also an English teacher, and it seems here that he thinks that because I offered him help, I see myself as above him. However, he still hasn't said what he wants, or why he has messaged me. So, I explain to him that I don't use chat.)

Me:
I only use chat for emergencies or close family, so I was confused.
Idea exchanges are on my regular page
(At this point, to my mind, the chat is over—he didn't know he was bothering me, but I've explained I don't use chat with strangers, so I am expecting him to either be silent or to say something like "Oh, excuse me.")

Stranger:
Are you interested in ELT
Ok My dear
(Now I'm more annoyed. Why is he asking if I'm interested in ELT? Did he not bother to read my profile before sending a friend request? Isn't that, in fact, why he sent one? I am also not happy with "My dear." For an American, that phrase is either patronizing or belittling, or romantic—and neither is appropriate here.)

Me:
Yes, I teach and write materials.
(I am doing my best to be neutral, although I am also hoping that by my terse answer, together with the fact that I have just explained I don't use chat except for family or emergencies, he will understand that I do not want to continue this chat.)

Stranger:
Can you send me a link to your page
I am English Teacher too
(*I am confused. What page? My Facebook page? Didn't he have to be on it, in order to send me a message?*)

Me:
I think if you can send a message you can access my profile. Sorry, plane boarding now
(*Not a lie—I really was busy!*)

And that was the end of it... for a month. And then:

Stranger:
Hi
How are you ?
(*How am I?! I am frustrated! I have already explained that I do not like this sort of intrusion. This clearly isn't someone who knows me, or who is interested in interacting in public on my page. I really don't know what he wants, but I feel very uncomfortable.*)

Me:
Please ... I don't use chat except for family members. Thank you for your understanding.
(*My one final plea. I don't know how I can express it more clearly...*)

Stranger:
What do you think yourself My dear ?
(*I don't actually know what he means here. I think, given the next exchange, that it's something like, "Who do you think you are, that*

you are too good to chat with me here?" But I am not sure. All I really know is, I have asked him more than once not to chat me, and he's not stopping. And he's calling me "My dear" again.)

Me:
If you don't stop messaging me, I will have to block you. Please stop.

Stranger:
I won't use either with unrespectful Like you

The conversation is now, thankfully, over—but it ended in disaster. He is angry and feels I have been disrespectful. I am angry and feel he has been disrespectful. But we are both EFL teachers, and I somehow can't help feeling that if we'd met face to face, we'd have gotten along well.

So what went wrong? My first guess is that it's mainly a cultural difference. In his culture, it must be OK to strike up conversations online with people you don't know, through private messaging. But in my culture, it's not. On my main page, in public, it's fine. But not in chat, and not in email either, if we don't know each other and have no business to conduct.

A further complication is our genders. I'd say almost all messages of this type come from men (I can think of only two women who ever tried this with me). A similar move from an American man would make me think it was someone looking for a date (someone who clearly hadn't checked my page and noticed that I am married). I wonder sometimes if my husband were to send chat messages out of the blue to their wives if that would go over well in their cultures. I suspect not, but I have never asked. But I have asked other Americans if they get chat messages like these, and overwhelmingly more women do (from men) than men do (from either gender).

When I am online, I am at work. I may have Facebook open, and post from time to time, but it's in between other websites loading or a spellcheck being run or email messages going back and forth about a project or waiting for a phone call. It's not, for me, 'dead time' where I have nothing to do, and am hoping someone might say "Hi" just to see what happens. I do have time for interesting discussions (usually!); but I don't have time to talk about nothing. I wonder if in some cultures being online at all is seen as someone's down time, when they are open to the world, for any type of communication.

I asked some other English teachers how they felt about messages from strangers.

> **British woman**: If it's just 'hi' I ignore it as I discovered that just politely saying I didn't use FB to chat with people I didn't already know did not work and just led to a lot more messages.

> **Canadian man**: If it seems like they specifically sought me out, have a real question, and are being appropriately polite, I'll answer. If it's just an empty "hi" I just ignore it.

> **German man**: I usually answer ... and then regret it. One answer from me seems to provoke just more and more questions.

British woman: I get quite a lot of 'hi' from people I haven't friended. I don't usually answer them, simply because it's distracting and I assume they just want to chat. They seem mainly to be male.

British man: If I haven't already friended them and they say Hi, how are you? I delete and block.

And then one American woman, not a teacher at all, contacted me because an EFL teacher connected to me had sent her a friend request, which she had accepted without thinking ... and then every time he saw her online, he would start sending her chat messages, one after the other:

> hi
> my dear
> how are u?
> good morning
> thx for accept my request
> hi

To an American, there is nothing there to respond to—no context, no content, no purpose and no interaction. It just feels like harassment.

Written communication, of course, like oral communication, is more than just words—it's habits and conventions and culture. Whose culture is it, though, on Facebook? No matter Facebook's country of origin, I don't see it as 'belonging' to any one culture or language anymore. However, if someone comes to my page, having invited himself, then I don't think it's unreasonable to at least try to be polite in my culture. If I were writing in French to someone who lived in France, I would do my best to write in ways that were appropriate to that culture (and if I didn't know what those were, I would try to find out).

Of course, anyone is free to interact on Facebook however he or she pleases. But I think most people want to be polite and want to make positive connections. I don't think they wish to be rude or to make other people feel intimidated or uncomfortable.

I have never seen an in-depth treatment of this topic—the culture of chat messages—in an ELT textbook. But I do think there's value in explicitly teaching the discourse, or at least raising the topic. As with any type of writing, it's a good opportunity to remind students to think of audience, purpose, and tone and register. People might not choose to alter their communication style—but they should at least know how they're being perceived.

Some teaching ideas:

- Print out this article, or portions of it, to read and discuss.
- Have students design a questionnaire or survey to check habits and attitudes—class, in the community, or online. They could post it on Facebook, for example.
- Brainstorm or present functional language for tasks such as addressing someone you don't know, politely interrupting in writing, and explaining your purpose or intention. Also teach phrases that may seem polite but can rub people

the wrong way (You know I'm thinking of *My dear!*).
- Have students interview someone from another culture, or someone whose social media style differs from their own, in depth, and explore the reasons behind the other person's feelings. Remind them that no one culture is "correct," but that for most people, harmonious interaction is the goal of chat.
- Present examples (authentic or made up) of "chats gone well"—conversations in writing where both participants felt they achieved something of value (an exchange of information, for instance, or warm feelings). These make good strip stories: print them, cut them apart, mix up the pieces of paper, and have students reconstruct the conversation.
- Examine and discuss the textual features of chat, such as a lack of capital letters and end punctuation, in some cases; line breaks to indicate a new thought or paragraph; abbreviations, emoticons, and stickers.

Note, however, that the cases I referred to in this article were not communications from students—they were communications from other teachers of English as a foreign language. The Internet and social media are so beneficial to our community of teachers. Let's continue to discuss with each other ways to keep it a safe and positive space in which to exchange ideas.

Food for thought: How do you feel about connection requests from strangers on social media? How about chats or direct messages? Have you ever sent a connection request to someone you didn't know? What was your purpose for doing so, and how was your request received?

15

SHE WAS IN A LIFT WITH A PRIEST WHO SNEEZED

You may be wondering what that title means.

I know I am.

And I wrote it.

I found this gem of wisdom in a stack of old conference

papers. A quick audience survey—how many teachers (and students) out there have that same stack of old conference papers? You know—handouts and notes you took at sessions at local, state, national, and international conferences. Yours might not be piled in a stack on the floor between two bookcases, like mine (which is not a system I recommend); perhaps yours are in the bottom of a box, or tucked inside folders and then filed in a cabinet, or perhaps they're in notebooks on your shelves.

But I bet you have them. Handouts, often on sheets of brightly colored paper so you'll (in theory) notice them more. Sheets of loose-leaf paper with your careful outlines at the top, then the notes you wrote to the person sitting next to you halfway down, and finally at the bottom some doodles that might be flowers. Some brochures might be in there, too, for new (at the time) textbooks and CDs, exciting grant opportunities, volunteer teaching abroad programs.

How many years do your stacks go back? Mine aren't too bad, if only because I moved around a lot, often from country to country, so I could thin things out each time I had to pay to ship my worldly possessions.

But I still have them. A few years ago I got inspired (if you want to call it that) and sorted many of them by subject area; so now I have a folder called "Reading," and another called "Culture," and another called "Grammar," and so on. These are then carefully arranged in a file cabinet drawer. And I go through those folders just as often as go the stack on the floor between the bookshelves.

Which is to say, never.

That's right. I feel a little nervous admitting this, but

I'm just going to make a clean breast of it: I never revisit those folders (unless I am filing more papers into them). I save those papers that I think are important, and when I sort through them, I make that decision again ("This is important! I'll need this someday!"), and then I file the papers away, and completely forget about them.

They're not really gone, of course. They're taking up physical space (a drawer and a half in my filing cabinet, and about 6 inches on the floor), and they're taking up mental space. Because I haven't really forgotten them, you see. I've forgotten the contents, sure, but not their existence. They live on in my semi-conscious, accusing me, reminding me that I was going to do something as soon as I got the time. Review the International Phonetic Alphabet. Finally figure out what neuro-linguistic programming was all about. Brush up on systemic functional grammar. Correlate state standards with my curriculum outcome goals. Why don't I just get a Ph.D. while I'm at it? And learn to bake bread?

I remember the year I stopped making handouts for my own conference presentations. It was in 2005, the year I started doing presentations on teacher burnout. Because you know what? I think handouts contribute to teacher burnout. They seem so important! We collect them and cart them home and then carry them around for years, feeling guilty each time we see them because we remember we never did go and look up all the web links in the reference section.

Now, I know some handouts are useful, at least to some audience members. I don't dispute that for a minute. But for everyone? At every talk? I can assure you too that when I tell audiences that they do not need to take notes, there is visible relief. Isn't it enough that you've given up another weekend (or even week) away from your family and friends and outside interests to come, in a sense, to work? We—presenters—are professional teachers. Can we not say something in an hour that will be inspiring and memorable, without making it a chore or assigning homework?

My policy on handouts now is this: If you want one, email me and I'll send it to you. Teachers do, sometimes—but then I think it's the teachers who actually want the handout and who really will do something with it. Fair enough. I do want my presentations to be useful.

I'm sure some teachers reading this will be arguing with me already. "But when I present on X, I need handouts! They're essential because ... " Well, fine, if they're essential, by all means create them and hand them out! I'm just asking that you think, really think, about what you need a handout for, and what you expect your audience to do with it. If it has links, perhaps it would be more welcome in an electronic document anyway, where teachers could easily click them. Perhaps it would be easier for your audience to store documents on their computers, so they could search for them later by key word or topic, rather than trying to remember in what city, in what year, they might have heard something about vocabulary.

I see more and more conferences, though, that say things to presenters like "Handouts are expected." Really? But you don't know my topic yet, or how I plan to present it. I don't have any wish to encourage paper collectors who won't actually be able to use what I give them.

Now, every presenter is different of course, and presents

on different topics, and in different ways. I've only told you how one person operates—me. So I'm interested in hearing from other teachers who attend conferences. Do you expect handouts? What do you do with your handouts when you get them? How do you store them? How often do you refer to them again?

Do you take notes when you attend presentations? What do you do with those notes? Are they useful to you later? Sometime in about, oh, 2008, I took notes at some conference, and I carefully noted down that title sentence: "She was in a lift with a priest who sneezed." At the time, it must have seemed important. In fact, it seemed important enough that I kept it for years. But why? What does it mean? I have no idea.

But I know what I just did with it.

I threw it away.

And it felt good.

Food for thought: How do you handle digital clutter—old documents and emails on your computer or email server? How often do you go through old material to organize or delete?

---

16. THE PLACE OF GAMES IN THE LANGUAGE CLASSROOM

I don't think it's any secret that I'm suspicious of classrooms whose goal is "fun," if that fun comes ahead of (or in place of...) actual learning. But I'm a huge fan of games. Is that a contradiction? Not at all—as long as your game serves a higher purpose.

What makes an activity a "game"? Often it's just how we dress it up. A game may be nothing more than extended pairwork asking and answering questions, but if it's done sitting around a game board, rolling dice, and moving markers, it's a game.

A time limit can make something a game: *How many vocabulary words from Unit 3 do you remember?* is just a question; *Work in groups of three. How many vocabulary words from Unit 3 can you list before the bell rings?* feels like a game.

When selecting or designing a game, I look for these factors:

- **It is useful.** That is, it is clearly practicing a language point or a communication skill. Not only must I be able to articulate that to myself, but I need to be able to explain it to my students as well.
- **Gameplay lasts longer than the instructions.** Some games might take a while to explain or learn or set up; in that case, the amount of practice students get needs to justify that.
- **It gives all students an equal amount of practice.** Games that rely purely on skill or knowledge can result in the stronger students getting more practice, and that of course is not fair. Be especially wary of games that have unsuccessful students sit down or stop play early, or that reward success with extra turns.

- **It does not cause hurt feelings.** Many games involve "winning" and "losing"—and losing is not usually such a great feeling for anyone. Therefore, the playing of the game itself must hold the appeal, not just the winning of it. When I have students of mixed abilities playing together, I don't mind at all altering the rules or outright "cheating" to level the playing field. A student normally cannot cheat without angering his/her classmates—but the teacher, now, she can do whatever she pleases! I give a specific example of this in the description of the flyswatter game.

I feel strongly that *your language goal* should be what drives you to select your game, and not the other way around. That is, if your language goal is *I want students to get to know each other better, feel comfortable in class, get some experience working in groups, and have some time for free conversation practice that isn't graded*, then the conversation game described in chapter one here would be a good fit for that class. However, it doesn't work nearly so well to say, *I have this great conversation board game, so… I guess 'conversation practice' will be my goal for my next class.*

The games described in this little book are ones I mostly made myself, with cardboard and paint and markers and cards and scissors. If you are making something that can be used more than once, I advise making the time and effort to do it well the first time, so it will last for years. If possible, laminate worksheets and flashcards. At the same time, keep your eye open for store sales and yard sales where you can pick up inexpensive game boards, dice, markers (I find little novelty erasers and coins from different countries work well), timers, and so on, so you can have them on hand when you suddenly have an inspiration for creating a game.

When you create a good game, write down the instructions so that another teacher could pick it up and use it. Make sure you note what levels it's good for and how long it takes to play. A game can make a wonderful tool for a substitute teacher if you are suddenly sick and aren't able to create a regular lesson plan.

And now... on to the games!

BOARD GAMES

Our first game is one of my all-time favorites. This conversation board game is easy to create, but one of the most useful ones I have in my magic bag of teacher supplies. It works with new classes as well as students who have been studying together for years. It works with children, adults, beginners, practically fluent students… even native speakers! If I were going into a completely unknown situation, this is the first thing I would take with me.

This works with private students as well as large classes, although do note that for large groups you will need several sets of materials.

If the game boards in the photos here look a bit beaten up, it's because I've been using them since 1992! The originals are made of heavy cardboard that was painted and then shellacked; the questions were written with permanent marker. I have also made color photocopies of the boards and had the copies laminated, so that I can roll them up and travel with them when necessary.

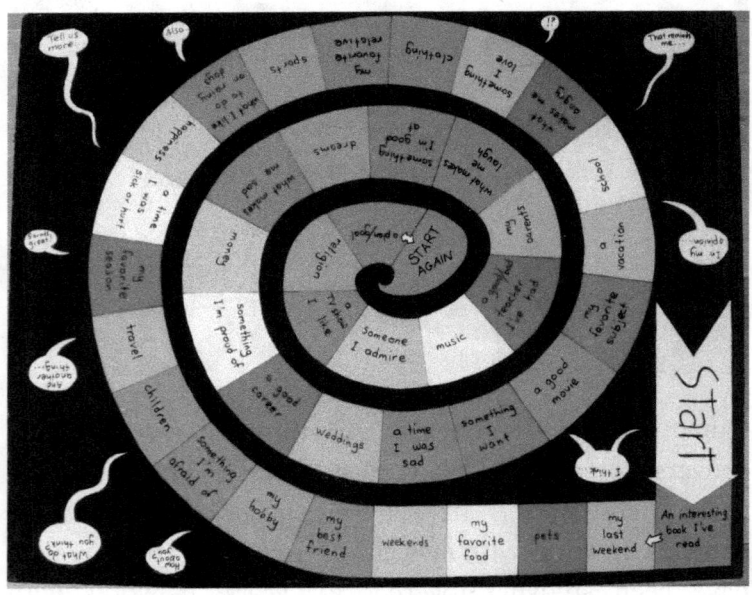

Simple game design with questions or prompts for topics.

The game is a merely a series of questions, such

as *What do you like to do on rainy days? What is something that makes you angry? How does your family celebrate birthdays?* I have simpler versions that feature only topics: *children, money, television, movies.*

Game board with single-word topics. This works well with lower-level students as well as upper-level ones. You can see the space that says "Africa" is a different color—that's actually a sticky note cut to the right shape stuck over the original, which said "Hawaii," because that's where I was living when I made the game. Over the years it's been changed to Asia, Europe, Africa, etc., depending on where I'm using it.

Students play in groups of 4-5 (more than that means that some students will fall silent).

All students in the group place a marker on start, and then they take turns to role a die and move their marker around the board. I buy the 8-, 9-, or 12-sided dice from hobby or gaming shops; if you don't have access to these, I recommend using two of the traditional six-sided dice. The higher the numbers they can roll, the more players will spread out around the board and land on different questions.

When a student lands on a question (or topic), she speaks about that topic *as much as she likes*. She can address any aspect of the topic; it is entirely her choice. The group members ask her questions, but do *not* offer their own answers or opinions. When the player feels she has finished, she passes the die or dice to the next student, and play continues. Everyone gets a turn asking questions as well as giving their own answers.

Two groups playing at different tables. Keep groups small enough that people have many chance to speak.

It's not a game that anyone can "win"—if someone

reaches the end of the path, the final square says "go back," and play reverses. I generally have students play for 20-30 minutes, but I have never had a group where any player got all the way back to start!

This is a wonderful game for the first day of class. Students get to know one another, and while they are playing, I walk around and listen to them—this is my evaluation of their English level. It provides solid practice in speaking, listening, and turn-taking. It's an extremely simple activity, and yet just having the questions in a "game" format makes it more interesting than the standard pair interview presented on a worksheet. I've frequently had classes request to play the game again during other sessions—and every time a group plays the game, or plays with different people, the game is different.

More complex questions can of course be designed that practice only the past tense, or conditional structures, or certain vocabulary, but I would mix that sort of question in with more general questions, so the game feels more like a fluency activity than a straight drill.

Blank game board for practicing grammar

This is a blank game board I've used for grammar games—this game takes more effort to create and prepare, but you can also consider having students make your game cards, or at least using the game over and over again if you are lucky enough to teach the same class for several terms.

This game board, as you can see, has nothing written on the squares other than a few simple game-play instructions not related to language; however, the squares are all painted one of six colors. Each color represents a type of task, and I create a stack of cards with the tasks on them. If you can find colored cards that match your game board, that's very nice, but if you can't, you can make a mark with a crayon, colored pencil, or marker on the top of the card to match the cards to the square.

Next, make up the tasks that go with the colors.

For example, yellow might indicate 'spell this word.' If a student lands on yellow, he draws a card and hands it to a fellow player without looking at it, and the other player asks him to spell the word. If he succeeds, he stays where he is; if he makes a mistake, he moves back one square.

Blue squares might ask a student to put a sentence in the present tense into the past; red could be 'unscramble this sentence'; green could be 'make this statement into a question', and so on. Make sure the grammar tasks are ones that students have already studied—this is a game that reviews grammar, not that teaches it!

You could even assign students in groups to come up with a series of tasks or exercises as homework, and then have each color represent a different group's cards.

Really, any type of drill-based language exercise can be put onto cards, where suddenly it becomes fun instead of boring. You needn't think up all of the exercises yourself, even—copy them out of your class textbook as a review. A student who has done Exercise 13 on page 143 doesn't want to do page 143 again. However, if items from Exercise 13 appeared on the backs of cards in a stack—well, you would be surprised at how happily students drill themselves with those items again and again!

I cannot get away from the issue of usefulness, however; and I would like to stress again that the purpose of any game must not only be clear to you but also clear to your students. You should always let a class know why they are doing what they are doing, and when the game is concluded, point out to them what language they practiced and how they practiced it.

Even teachers enjoy playing the conversation game!

FLYSWATTERS

This vocabulary review game is a good one for large classes, and because it is active, it's also a good one for waking up sleepy classes or injecting a bit of energy into a lesson.

I first saw this game demonstrated at a monthly JALT (Japan Association of Language Teachers) meeting in Chiba in… 1988? and I'm afraid I can no longer remember the name of the presenter. But thank you so much, whoever you were!

To play requires flashcards with words or pictures, and at least two flyswatters. If you check a variety store or even a grocery store at the beginning of summer, you can probably find cheap flyswatters in bright colors and interesting designs.

For the flashcards, use words that students have already studied, or that you can pre-teach before the game begins. You can buy commercially made flashcards, but equally well cut pictures out of magazines or download images from the Internet, draw pictures by hand, or have students draw pictures for you, either in class or as homework.

The class is divided into two teams. A large class might require two or more separate games, but each team can easily have 6-10 members (and the number doesn't need to be the same on each team), because play moves very quickly.

The teams gather on opposite sides of a large table, and the flashcards are scattered all over the table.

One representative from each team steps up to the table, flyswatter in hand. The teacher (or, later, a student leader) can, at the lowest level, simply call out the name of the object on the card. The first student to smack the correct card with the flyswatter "wins" the card and one point for the team. (And now you see why we use flyswatters—they can reach any point on the table, and it doesn't hurt when the person from the other team smacks down on top!).

A student swats the correct word.

The person who wins the card hands her flyswatter to the next person on her team and moves to the end of the line or group (I don't think I've ever had a class manage to stay in a single-file line–they get too excited and want to crowd around the table watching).

The person from the other team who "lost" remains in place for a maximum of two more plays. In this way, an unsuccessful student gets more chances than a successful student—presumably, they need the practice more. But even an unsuccessful student is not put on the spot for very long. Whether a team wins or loses doesn't depend on one person, which also reduces the pressure for each student.

When you call out a word, make sure you do not look directly at the card you are referring to, or students will simply follow your eyes! Pick the card you want, and then look away as you say the word or sentence.

Waiting for the word to be called. As you can see, it's crucial to have a flat space. This narrow table isn't as convenient as a wider one, but it was good enough for our purposes.

Here is a game that is easy for the teacher to "fix"—if one team is winning by too great a margin, I might do something like call out the card and then simply hold the arm of the player of the winning team, or cover his eyes. In this way, the player from the other team has all the time necessary to locate the card. If you are very obvious about it, the class will accept it. After all, you have made it clear from the beginning what the purpose of the activity is—

practicing vocabulary recognition. That is always the goal, and not "winning."

You'll notice that even though only one person plays for a team at each time, the entire team will crowd around the table to watch; even though they are observers, they are just as focused on the vocabulary as the players. You might need to remind them a few times not to point or "help" the person playing! But they will certainly be rehearsing the vocabulary in their heads.

After 7-10 minutes of play, in fact, I like to stop the game and point this out to students, and ask them to notice how engaged they are and how focused on the vocabulary they are even when it is not their turn. In this way, the students know that their time is not being wasted.

If you find that students are, in their enthusiasm, randomly slapping cards hoping to get lucky, rather than actually locating the correct card, impose a "return one card to the table for every incorrect slap" penalty.

A student takes over calling out the words and sentences.

To increase the difficulty level, you can say whole sentences with the words in them, or even short paragraphs or longer stories; you can describe the word without giving it directly; and so on.

The flashcards needn't be picture cards—they can be

single letters for young learners, or even complex linguistic terms for graduate students (for which you give a definition or example).

If you wish to have picture cards but don't have the time to create your own, why not assign the task to students? Give each student or group a certain amount of vocabulary and some blank cards, and let them draw pictures or find them from magazines or the Internet and glue the images onto the cards. If you can, then laminate the cards so they will last longer, and keep them for use in future classes as well.

The game may seem as though it is designed for children, with cards and flyswatters and constant motion, and certainly children love this game (it's an excellent way to review colors, letters of the alphabet, and numbers). However, I've used it with teacher trainers and company employees and university students and other groups, who enjoyed it immensely. Adults love games too!

CONCENTRATION

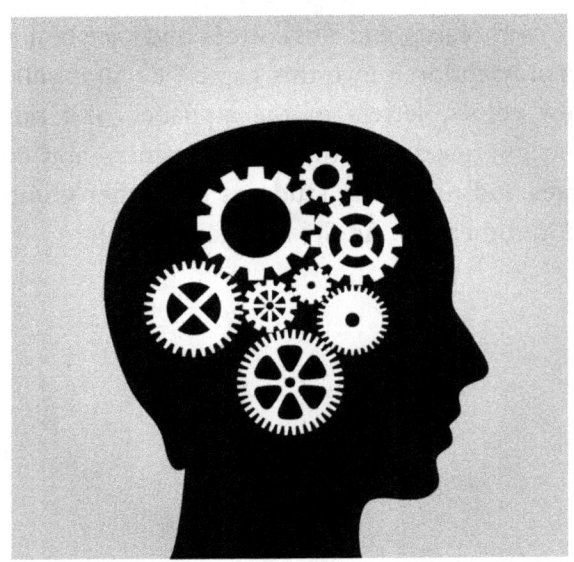

Many students will already know this classic matching game, also sometimes called "Memory" or "Pelmanism," but even if they don't, it's not hard to explain.

I use this game as an intensive vocabulary review,

for words I want students to have as active vocabulary that they can use, not just passive vocabulary that they can recognize. Allow a good 45 minutes! And with the extension activities listed at the end, it can fill an hour. However, if the preparation is done the class before or as homework, it can be played in 20 minutes.

Students are divided into groups of 4-6. If time permits (here is the step that can be done as homework), each group is given 20-25 words or allowed to choose words from their textbook or other source they have used. Words should be ones previously studied, however; this is a review game, not a teaching game. Students write a definition of the word or an original sentence that exemplifies the word, with a blank line where the word would go.

Example: the target word is "luxury"

For me, a cell phone is not a _____ . It's an essential tool for my personal and professional life.

It's important that you check each sentence or definition to make sure it is correct and sufficient, since the group will be drilling with these sentences.

When the definitions and sentences have been approved, students write the word on a small blank flashcard (I cut standard 3" x 5" file cards in half) and the matching definition or sentence on another.

The words are shuffled together, and the sentences and definitions are shuffled together.

The cards are then laid face down in rows. If you are playing with 25 vocabulary words, then you will have 5 rows of 5 cards on one side of the table for the words, and more practice, whereas it is really the weaker students who need more practice, so I don't allow it.

Inevitably, cards will be drawn again and again, even after their matches have been seen before. This is the nature of the drill — students are repeating and remembering, repeating and remembering. It may take some supervision on your part to remind them to say the words and definitions/sentences aloud *each time*, yet this is the crucial step.

The game finishes when all cards have been matched.

I have noticed that some groups play competitively, with each student trying to win the most cards. Other groups play more cooperatively, and even though they take turns drawing the cards, other members will give suggestions or help out. It doesn't matter which way they play, as they get just as much practice either way, so I let groups determine for themselves how to conduct that aspect of the game.

if you give different groups different colors of cards, it's easy to keep the games organized, and depending on the words chosen, groups can even swap games and play another group's game during a different class.

If time remains in class, have students make two stacks of cards, again keeping the words together and the definitions/sentences together. First, have them take turns drawing a definition/sentence and recalling the words (they should be pleasantly surprised by how easy this is!).

Then, have them take turns drawing a word and either recalling the example definition/sentence or creating a new one. This, too, is usually pretty easy by this point.

Students of all ages and levels enjoy this game, and the advantage for you is that they will drill and drill until they really know the words, with minimal supervision on your part. You can even keep the games the groups have created to use with other classes (as long as those other classes are studying the same vocabulary, of course). Cutting out the preparation step means less practice for new groups, but does save the preparation time.

For beginners, use one set of cards with images and the other set with the words (tomato, corn, etc.). The student reads the word card aloud, and then tries to remember the name of the image—if he can't, other group members help. Very low-level students could read the English word and identify the vegetable in the picture in their native language.

www.ingramcontent.com/pod-product-compliance
Lightning Source LLC
Chambersburg PA
CBHW060813050426
42449CB00008B/1650